AF412562

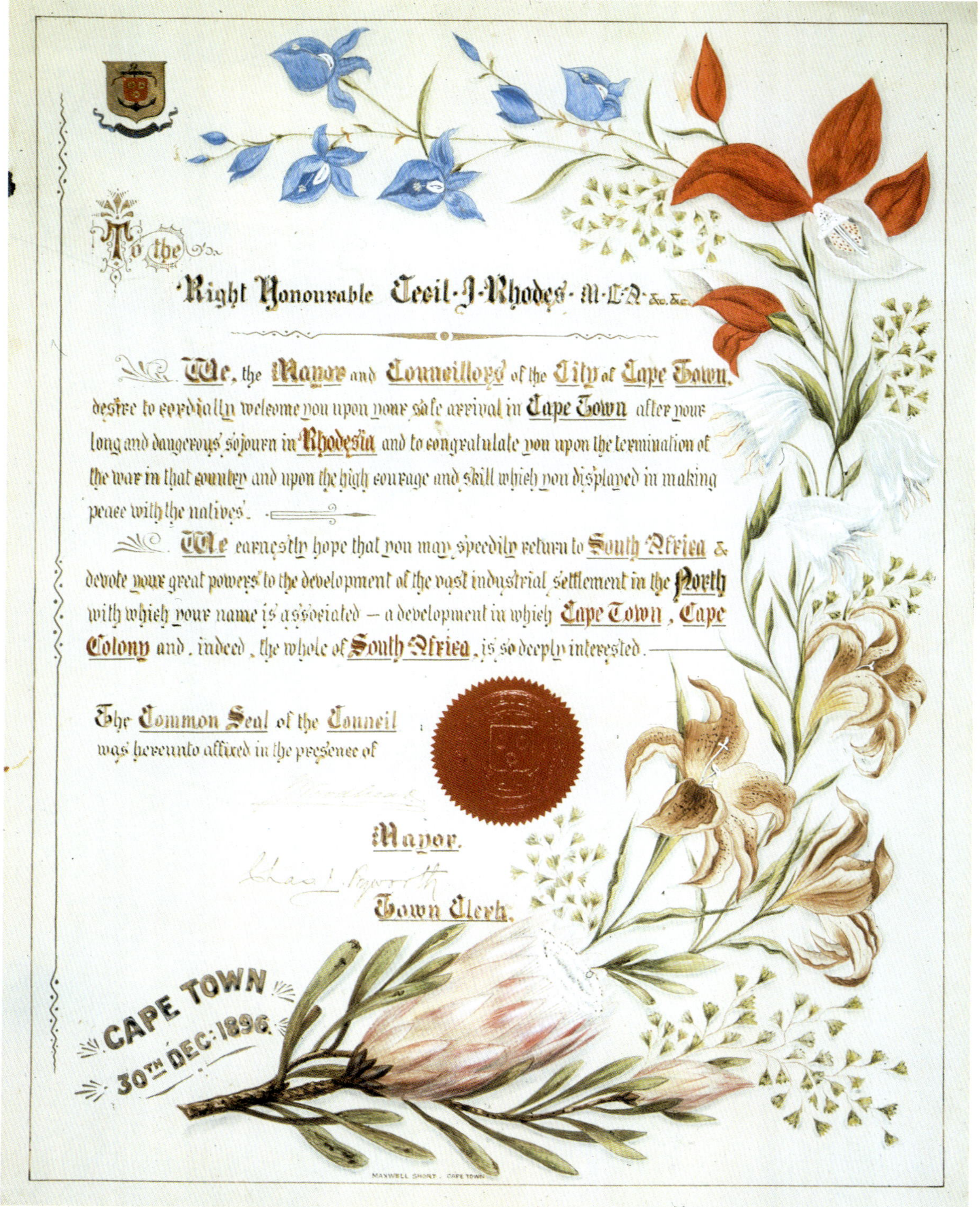

Illuminated address presented to Cecil Rhodes. (Item 2)

SOUTH AFRICA
IN THE TWENTIETH CENTURY

FROM BOER WAR TO AMANDLA!

AN EXHIBITION AT THE BODLEIAN LIBRARY
SPRING 2000

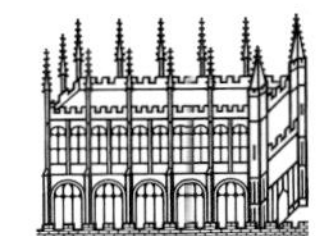

Bodleiar Library
University of Oxford

Outside front cover: items 7, 76, 122.

Outside back cover: item 110.

Inside front & back covers: item 17.

© 2000 Bodleian Library, University of Oxford.

ISBN 1-85124-064-0

Designed and typset in Gill Sans by Graham Wilkins
at the Bodleian Library, Oxford.

Printed by Cheney and Sons Ltd., Banbury.

Acknowledgements

The Library wishes to express its thanks to
Anglo-American Corporation for their most
generous support of the exhibition, which,
amongst other things, has made possible
the publication of the exhibition catalogue.

This exhibition and the accompanying
catalogue have been created through the
collaboration of the following members of
the Bodleian Library staff: John Pinfold and
Lucy McCann (Rhodes House Library),
Dana Josephson and Alison McKay (Preservation
& Conservation Department), Joanna Dodsworth
and Graham Wilkins (Marketing & Publishing
Division), Julie Anne Lambert (John Johnson
Collection), Jackie Merralls (Photographic Studio)
and Penny Sturgis (South African Friends of the
Bodleian).

We are most grateful to Ian Phimister
(St. Cross College) for his help and advice,
and especially for writing the historical parts
of the catalogue.

Thanks are also due to the following for their
help and assistance in planning the exhibition:
the Rhodes Trust, Robin Fryde, Helen Kimble,
Donal Lowry, Ian Shapiro, Cecillie Swaisland and
Philip Waller.

Contents

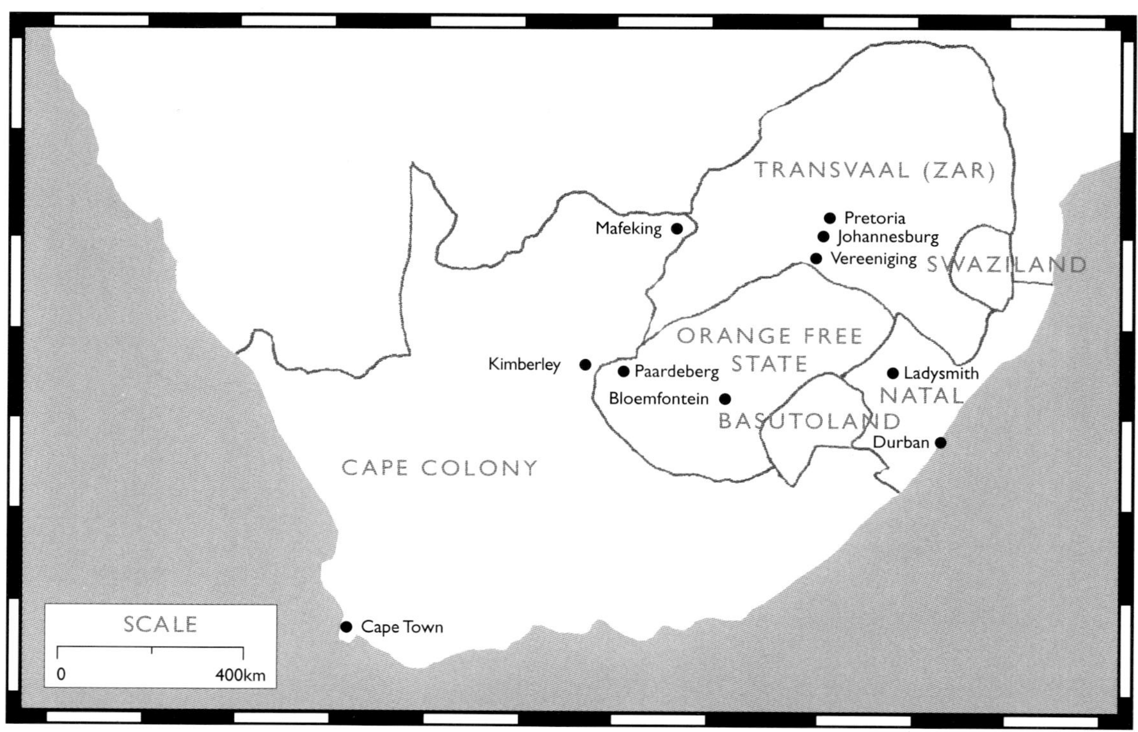

South Africa at the time of the Anglo-Boer War

RHODES, THE RAND AND THE ANGLO-BOER WAR

For much of the last fifteen years or so of the nineteenth century the dominant figure in Southern Africa was Cecil Rhodes (1853-1902). Mining tycoon, colonial politician and imperial visionary, Rhodes has been succinctly described as an unprincipled opportunist of genius, whose dream was 'the furtherance of the British Empire and the bringing of the whole uncivilized world under British rule'. The wealth and political power which enabled Rhodes if not to rule the world, at least to shape the destiny of the sub-continent, were based on the amalgamation of Kimberley's diamond fields. While never enjoying complete control either over the sale of diamonds or over the profits of the newly-consolidated De Beers Company, Rhodes nonetheless insisted that its trust deed should permit the acquisition of 'any asset of any kind by any means'.

Most famously, Rhodes used De Beers to underwrite the northern operations of his British South Africa Company at the start of the 1890s. As soon as it became clear that his Gold Fields of South Africa Company had ended up with some of the poorest sections of the recently discovered Witwatersrand goldfield in the Transvaal, Rhodes pinned his hopes on finding a 'Second Rand' in the region between the Limpopo and Zambezi rivers. In this he had Britain's backing, as the magnitude of the gold deposits on the Rand began to tilt the balance of economic and political power away from the Cape Colony towards President Kruger's Boer republic. Britain's supremacy, it appeared, was at stake.

By 1894, however, prospectors had failed to locate a comparable goldfield in either Mashonaland or Matabeleland. Instead, mining engineers proved beyond doubt that the real 'Second Rand' actually lay beneath the first one, in what were termed its 'deep levels'. But not only was the Transvaal immeasurably richer than had previously been supposed, the taxation and concessions policies of its government pressed most heavily on those mining companies which were increasingly bound up with the very costly business of extracting gold ore from thousands of feet underground. It was in this context that the Jameson Raid, 'a desperate and thoroughly mismanaged conspiracy organized by Rhodes and a group of close associates, many of whom had links with deep level mining', was launched in December 1895.

Rhodes' raiders were easily defeated. It was soon suspected that Imperial officials in Cape Town and London, up to and including the Colonial Secretary, Joseph Chamberlain, had all been involved in the plot to overthrow Kruger's regime. Boer mistrust of the British intensified, especially once Chamberlain appointed Sir Alfred Milner, an ardent imperialist, as High Commissioner at the Cape in May 1897. For both sides the whole question of whether the wealth of the Transvaal would ultimately give rise to a United States of South Africa outside the British Empire, or to a confederation of states on the Canadian model, loyal to Britain, revolved on the voting rights of the immigrant 'Uitlander' population attracted to the mines. Although the relative size of the Afrikaner and Uitlander population, most of whom were British, must remain a matter of conjecture as no census was conducted before the war, it does seem likely that there were more Uitlander than Afrikaner adult males. Fearing the probable electoral consequences of this state of affairs, Kruger restricted the Uitlander franchise to naturalized citizens who had lived in the Transvaal for fourteen years, while Milner, acting in concert with disaffected Randlords, pushed hard for the enfranchisement of what he famously described as Johannesburg's 'helot' British population.

British policy was based on the assumption that when push came to shove the Boers would give way. No-one appears to have been unduly concerned when the negotiations broke down at the Bloemfontein Conference in June 1899, and it was not until September that troops were belatedly dispatched to reinforce existing British garrisons in South Africa. However, the Transvaal, joined by the Orange Free State, decided to strike before it was too late. An ultimatum demanding the withdrawal of British troops was followed in October and November 1899 by Boer attacks on Natal and the Cape Colony. During 'Black Week' of 10-17 December 1899, British arms suffered a series of humiliating reverses, notably at Magersfontein and Colenso. Yet by laying siege to Kimberley, Ladysmith and Mafeking, Boer commandos squandered tactical mobility and strategic initiative, even as fresh Imperial troops poured into South Africa. Now under the command of Lords Roberts and Kitchener, British troops entered Johannesburg at the end of May 1900, and captured Pretoria less than a week later. The war, it seemed, would soon be over. In fact it was to continue for almost another two years. Drawing novel conclusions from the British advance, the Boers now waged a hit-and-run guerrilla campaign against their slow-moving adversary. British forces, eventually totalling around 450,000 troops in all, struck back by burning farms and crops, slaughtering livestock and driving Boer women, children and servants into concentration camps. Extensively employed on each warring side, despite claims to the contrary, many Africans took advantage of the conflict to reclaim their lost lands. With this ominous development gathering pace, Boer and British leaders signed the Treaty of Vereeniging in May 1902. If the fiction of a 'white man's war' was not to be fatally exposed, then a 'white man's peace' had urgently to be made.

Cecil Rhodes

Prime Minister of the Cape Colony, until forced to resign following the fiasco of the Jameson Raid, Rhodes was responsible for British expansion into Matabeleland and Mashonaland (present-day Zimbabwe) and sought to gain control of the gold-rich Boer republic of the Transvaal.

1 Portrait of Cecil Rhodes by Cecil Cutler, 1900. *Rhodes House Library: Mss. Afr. s. 2201/7*

2, 3 Two illuminated addresses presented to Cecil Rhodes, one by the Cape Town

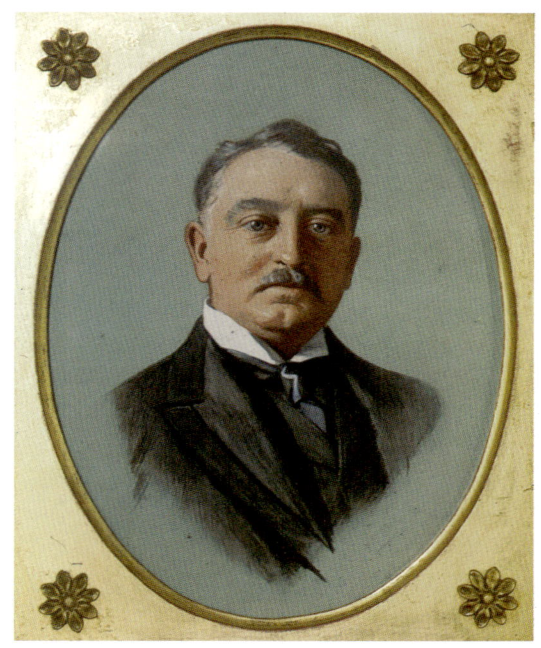

1

Municipality in 1896, and the second by the Cape Coloured community in 1899, following his return from Germany where he met Kaiser Wilhelm II, signed an agreement to establish a telegraph route through German East Africa and discussed the projected building of the Cape to Cairo railway. The latter is interesting in showing that the Coloured community at that period looked to Rhodes as their political leader. *Rhodes House Library: Rhodes papers*

Gold

Gold was discovered on the Rand in the late 1880s, and by the following decade it was clear that the wealth of the mines would transform the backward Boer republic of the Transvaal, led by President Paul Kruger, into the economic powerhouse of southern Africa. In the 1890s there was a Gold Rush as immigrants from Europe and North America flocked to Johannesburg. Although it was the issue of exclusion of the 'Uitlanders' from political rights which led to a breakdown in relations between the British government and the Transvaal, there can be little doubt that an underlying cause of the Anglo-Boer War was the question of who should control the great mineral wealth of the Rand.

4 *Scenes and life in the Transvaal* (London, *ca.* 1895), opened to show an early underground photograph of a gold mine on the Rand.
Rhodes House Library: 623.11 s.8

5 F.H. Hatch & J.A. Chalmers. *The gold mines of the Rand* (London, 1895), opened to show a diagram of a gold mine.
Rhodes House Library: 623.14 s.3

Popular reactions to the Anglo-Boer War

The Anglo-Boer War generated a large amount of public interest and controversy, and great numbers of commemorative items were produced at the time, a selection of which are displayed here. The lantern slide lectures were used to boost morale at home in the same way as newsreels were to be used during later conflicts, and indeed the Anglo-Boer war was the first of Britain's wars to be captured on film. After the war, there were re-enactments of some of the major engagements, in which many of the actual participants, including some of the Boer generals, took part.

6 Transvaal money-box in the shape of a caricature of President Kruger, *ca.*1900.
Private collection

7 Character jug of Field Marshal Lord Roberts, *ca.*1900.
Private collection

8 Staffordshire figure of Lord Kitchener on horseback, *ca.* 1901.
Private collection

9 Bet made between Sammy Marks and Mr.
Coffey on 5 October 1899, a week before
hostilities broke out, as to whether the South
African Republic would still be in existence in
a year's time.
Rhodes House Library: Mss Afr. r.250

10 F. & J. Smith's *Boer war series*. Cigarette card
album, *ca.* 1900.
Bodleian Library: John Johnson Collection:
M.L. Horn cigarette card collection, Military 1

11, 12 *The Transvaal War*. Sets of lantern slides
and lecture notes, 1900.
Rhodes House Library: Mss. Afr. r.249 and
Mss. Afr. s.2238

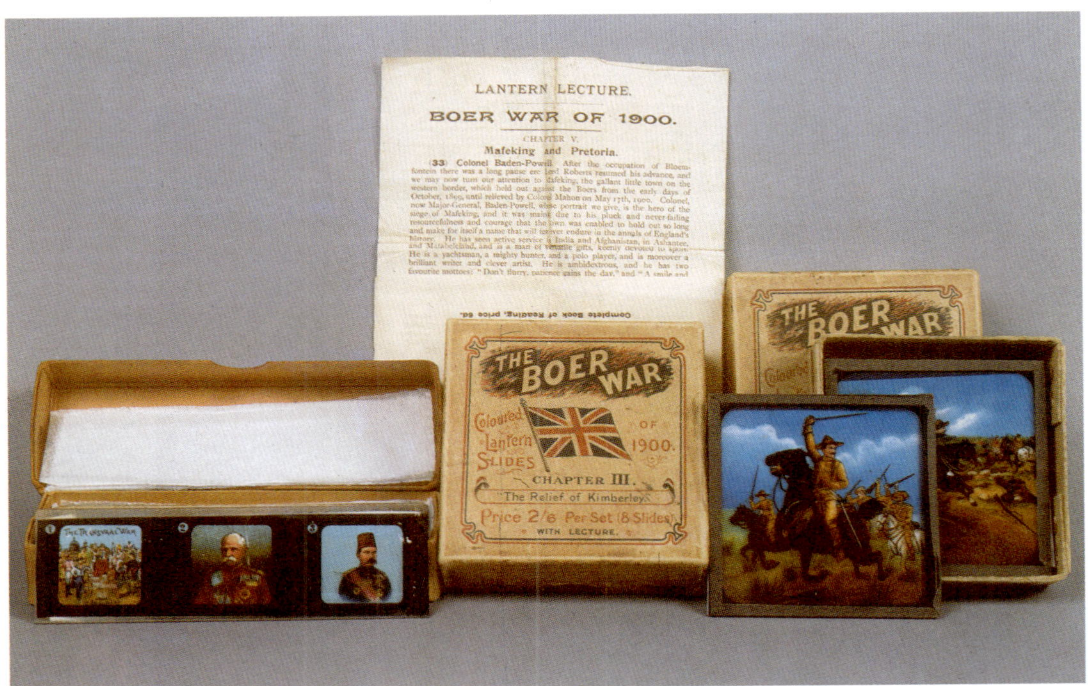

11, 12

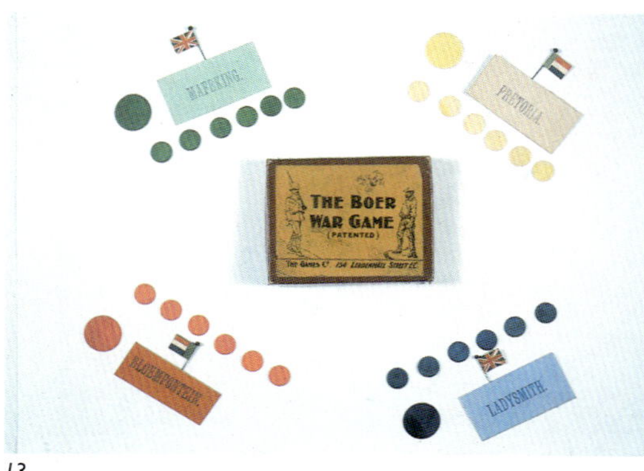

13

Images and Artefacts of the war

17 Flag of the C.I.V. (City Imperial Volunteers),
ca. 1900.
Private collection

18 Frank Rhodes' photograph album of the
Anglo-Boer War
Frank Rhodes was the elder brother of Cecil
Rhodes. A soldier who had served in the Sudan,
India and Ireland, as well as southern Africa,
during the Anglo-Boer War he was in the Siege
of Ladysmith and later took part in the relief of
Mafeking. The album is opened to show some of
his photographs of Mafeking, including an unusual
shot of Baden-Powell.
Rhodes House Library: Mss. Afr. s.2201/4

13 Boer War game, *ca.* 1900.
*Bodleian Library: John Johnson Collection: Games
drawer 25*

14 *The Absent-minded beggars at war in Africa.*
Printed handkerchief, 1899.
*Bodleian Library: John Johnson Collection:
Printed fabrics 6 (Roger Warner donation)*

15 Stephen Downes. *Paul Kruger's doom.*
Printed poem, 1899.
*Bodleian Library: John Johnson Collection:
South African War box 2*

16 Official programme for the Anglo-Boer War
Historical Libretto, staged at the World's Fair,
St. Louis, U.S.A., 1904.
Rhodes House Library: C99.R840

19 Jeppe's Map of the Transvaal, 1899
This series of maps, compiled from surveys filed
in the Surveyor General's Office in Pretoria, was
regarded as the most detailed and authoritative
available, and many British officers sought to obtain
them in preference to the official army maps.
Rhodes House Library: 623.11 r.10

20 Anglo-Boer War shell
This Boer shell is reputed to be the last one
fired at the siege of Mafeking.
Lent by the Rhodes Trust

21 Souvenir of the Siege of Kimberley
Queen Victoria's chocolate box, surrounded by
portraits of General French, Field Marshal Lord
Roberts, Colonel Kekewich, H.A. Oliver (the
Mayor of Kimberley), and Cecil Rhodes, *ca.*1900.
Private collection

22 President Kruger of the Transvaal
As a boy, Kruger took part in the Great Trek and
witnessed the Battle of the Blood River in 1838.
Brought up as a strict Calvinist (it is said he never
read any book other than the Bible), he first
became President of the Transvaal in 1883. In
1895-96 his astute handling of the Jameson Raid
severely embarrassed the British government
and led to the resignation of Cecil Rhodes as
Prime Minister of the Cape. Determined to resist
Milner's imperialism, he led the Transvaal into the
Anglo-Boer War, but his age and ill-health meant
effective leadership passed to other hands as
the war progressed. He remained in Pretoria
until a few days before its capture, then fled to
Portuguese East Africa (Mozambique) before
travelling on to Europe. He died in exile in
Switzerland in 1904.
Vanity Fair cartoon, 1900.
Rhodes House Library

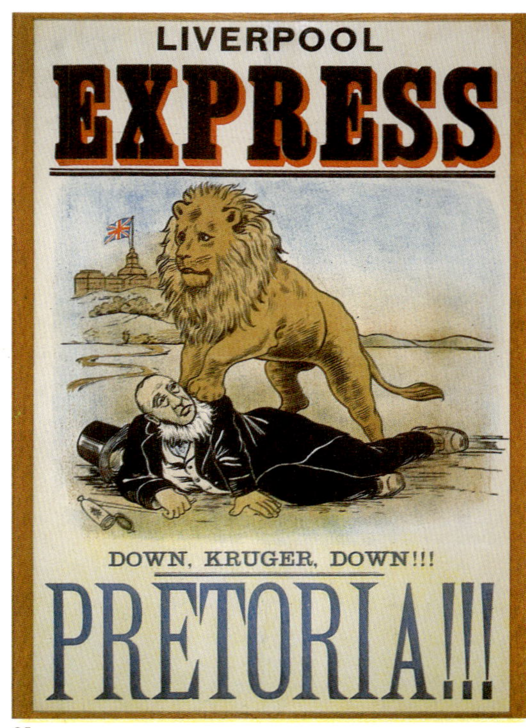

25

23 President Steyn of the Orange Free State
Steyn was a moderate who attempted to
mediate between the British and the Transvaal
government before the outbreak of the Anglo-
Boer War. Once the war began he felt bound to
honour his country's military alliance with the
Transvaal, and as the war progressed he proved
to be a more effective leader than President
Kruger. After the war he worked to reconcile

the British and the Boers, and played a part in bringing about the creation of the Union of South Africa in 1910. He died in 1916.
Vanity Fair cartoon, 1900.
Rhodes House Library

24 Mafeking Relieved
Liverpool Echo poster, 1900.
On loan to Rhodes House Library

25 Pretoria!!!
Liverpool Evening Express poster, 1900.
On loan to Rhodes House Library

Siege of Ladysmith

Militarily, Ladysmith was a far more important siege than Mafeking, and it was also more costly. Following the early reverses suffered by Sir George White's forces, approximately 21,300 people were besieged in the town, of whom 13,500 were soldiers. By the time Ladysmith was relieved on 28 February 1900 after a siege of 118 days, the British had suffered around 7000 casualties in the attempt, General Buller fighting four battles, including the disasters at Colenso and Spion Kop, before succeeding.

26 Printed list of food and tobacco prices at Ladysmith during the siege, 1900.
Rhodes House Library: Mss. Afr. r.245

27 *The Ladysmith Lyre*, 27 November 1899, open to show a drawing by Lionel James of an interrupted cricket match during the siege. Note the amount of 'True news' reported.
Rhodes House Library: James papers

28 Photograph of a cricket team composed of newspaper correspondents, Ladysmith, 1900.
Rhodes House Library: James papers

29 The Christmas number of *The Ladysmith bombshell*, 1899.
Rhodes House Library: 610.16 s.4

30 H. Kisch. *Photographs of the siege of Ladysmith* (n.p., 1900)
Bodleian Library: 24691 d.17

31 Letter from Lionel James, *The Times* correspondent in Ladysmith, to his wife, with home-made envelope, January 1900. Letters such as this were smuggled out of Ladysmith during the siege, using African boys as runners. This was an extremely hazardous undertaking, and the fact the series of letters is incomplete suggests that not all the runners employed by James got through.
Rhodes House Library: James papers

Siege of Kimberley

With a population of 50,000, Kimberley was much larger than either Mafeking or Ladysmith. It also contained the major prizes of the diamond mines and of Cecil Rhodes himself, who went there immediately before the outbreak of war, despite, or perhaps because of the Boers' threats to parade him in a cage through Pretoria if he was captured. The town suffered a siege of 124 days, being relieved on 15 February 1900, as part of the preliminaries before the battle of Paardeberg.

32 Photograph of Cecil Rhodes outside the Sanatorium, Kimberley, 1900.
Rhodes House Library: Rhodes papers

33 Photograph of a British shell fired during the siege of Kimberley, marked 'Compts. C.J.R.', December 1899.
Rhodes House Library: James papers

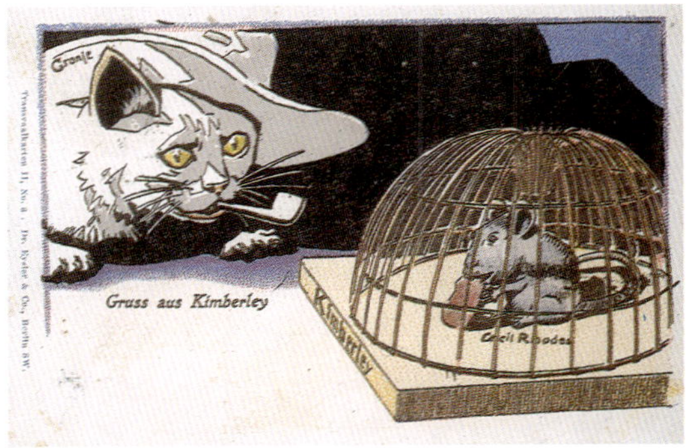

34

34 German postcard depicting Rhodes as a rat in a cage, watched by General Cronje as the cat, 1900. The card was posted in Vienna on 6 February 1900.
Rhodes House Library: Mss. Afr. r.256

35 Recollections of Edgar Sheppey, who was in charge of the horses and other livestock owned by De Beers, opened to show Rhodes' reaction to horse soup, and his impatience with his employees. Sheppey's account confirms that of others that, during the siege, Rhodes was 'a difficult man to please'.
Rhodes House Library: Mss. Afr. s.102

36 Siege diary of Mrs. Sheppey, opened to show her reaction to the order that all women and children were to take refuge from the shelling by going down the mines. Mrs. Sheppey was later the first woman to greet the relieving force – '14,000 glorious fellows' – when it finally arrived.
Rhodes House Library: Mss. Afr. s.102

37 Recollections of Mrs. Hemming, manageress of the Sanatorium, where Rhodes stayed during the siege of Kimberley. These were written down *ca.* 1950.
Rhodes House Library: Mss. Afr. s.69/2 item 3

Siege of Mafeking

Mafeking was besieged from October 1899. Defended by both white and African forces, commanded by Baden-Powell, it held out until relieved in May 1900. This was achieved by reducing rations, especially for the Africans, to a minimum and by driving many of the African non-combatants out of the town to fend for themselves. The relief of the town after a siege of 217 days was greeted with great jubilation in England, even giving rise to a new word, to 'maffick', meaning 'to exult riotously'.

38 *Mafeking Mail*, the newspaper printed inside the town during the siege.
Rhodes House Library: 610.16 t.2

39 D. Taylor. *Souvenir of the siege of Mafeking* (Mafeking, 1900).
Rhodes House Library: C99.S00126

40 Edward Garraway's diary of the relief of Mafeking, open to show the entry for 17 May, the day the town was relieved. Garraway served with Plumer's column, which approached Mafeking from the north.
Rhodes House Library: Mss. Afr. s.1610/3 item 7

Alfred, Viscount Milner

41 Milner was appointed High Commissioner for South Africa in 1897, and his imperialist policies have been regarded by many as the prime cause of the Anglo-Boer War. Following the end of the war in 1902 he was appointed administrator of the two defeated Boer republics. He created a team of talented young officials (known as 'Milner's Kindergarten') who worked to restore the political and economic infrastructure of the country. However, he mishandled the issue of 'Chinese slavery' and his acceptance of the report of the South African Native Affairs Commission meant that Africans would continue to be excluded from political and economic power. Milner returned to England in 1906. He subsequently served in the War Cabinet during the First World War.
Portrait by Sir James Guthrie.
Lent by the Rhodes Trust

A Soldier's Experience of the War

The Anglo-Boer War was the first war to be fought by a newly literate working class, following the education reforms of 1870, and consequently for the first time many rank and file soldiers were able to write home describing their experiences.

With what seems in hindsight an extraordinary lack of censorship, they were able to be openly critical of the way the war was being waged and of their officers, and their letters are full of complaints about poor food, boots falling to pieces and conditions generally.

42 Two letters of Walter Barley, dated 9 June and 13 July 1900. Barley was a painter and decorator from Lincolnshire, and was a member of K Company, 1st Rifle Battalion (Lincoln), Lincolnshire Rifle Volunteers, serving in South Africa from February 1900 to May 1901. His letters reveal the everyday concerns of lack of food and poor quality equipment, especially boots. They also record that, perhaps fortunately for him, he missed one battle by getting lost on the way. It is interesting to note that the letters are written in Lincolnshire dialect.
Rhodes House Library: Barley papers

43 Photograph of K Company, 1st Rifle Battalion (Lincoln) in South Africa, 1900. Walter Barley is first on the right, front row.
Rhodes House Library: Barley papers

44 Chocolate tin, 1899-1900. Queen Victoria sent a tin to each soldier in South Africa. The lid carries an embossed portrait of the Queen, with the message 'I wish you a happy New Year' and the inscription 'South Africa 1900'. This tin still contains the original chocolate.
Private collection

Battle of Paardeberg

The battle of Paardeberg, at the conclusion of which General Cronje surrendered to Lord Roberts, represented the first major defeat for the Boer forces. Following it, Roberts was able to resume his march into the Orange Free State and occupy its capital, Bloemfontein, on 13 March 1900.

45 *The Anglo-Boer War, 1899-1900: an album of upwards of three hundred photographic engravings* (Cape Town, *ca.* 1900)
Rhodes House Library: 610.16 s.9

46 Photograph of General Cronje after the surrender at Paardeberg.
Rhodes House Library: Lee papers

47 Tea cup commemorating the surrender of General Cronje at Paardeberg, *ca.* 1900.
Private collection

48 Letter from Lord Roberts to Cecil Rhodes, written the day after the surrender of Cronje, requesting further supplies of biscuits and forage. A postscript states 'I hope to reach Kimberley tomorrow morning, so please don't come here'.
Rhodes House Library: Mss. Afr. r.254

The Invasion of the Transvaal

Roberts' force crossed the Vaal River on 26 May 1900. Johannesburg surrendered on 30 May, its mines still intact despite fears of sabotage, and on 5 June Roberts entered Pretoria. Thereafter the Boers employed guerrilla tactics to continue the war, to which the British responded with a policy of farm burning and establishing a network of blockhouses, linked by barbed wire, to try to contain the Boer commandos.

49 Copy of the *Pretoria Friend*, the official military newspaper.
Rhodes House Library: 610.16 t.1

50 French postcard with a printed appeal for peace in South Africa, addressed to the Russian Tsar Nicholas II as convenor of the Hague Convention, *ca.* 1900. It depicts Kruger as Christ carrying a cross away from burning buildings, a reference to the scorched earth tactics employed by Roberts and Kitchener.
Rhodes House Library: Mss. Afr. r.263

51 Photograph of a Boer farm being burned by British troops.
Rhodes House Library: Lee papers

52 Three photographs of British blockhouses, *ca.* 1900.
Rhodes House Library: Mss. Afr. r.264

Winston Churchill and the Anglo-Boer War

Winston Churchill went out to South Africa as war correspondent for the *Morning Post*. On 15 November 1899, whilst riding on an armoured train near Chieveley, he was captured by some of Louis Botha's troops. His subsequent escape from captivity in Pretoria brought him instant fame, and contributed to his first becoming elected to Parliament as member for Oldham in 1900. Churchill's own account of his escape in *London to Ladysmith* and subsequently *My early life* has become the accepted version of events, although many people at the time, as Trooper Lowe's diary shows, were sceptical and felt Churchill had been allowed to escape by the Boers.

53 Mortimer Menpes. *War impressions* (London, 1901), opened to show a sketch of Churchill as war correspondent.
Rhodes House Library: 610.16 r.81

54 Winston Spencer Churchill. *London to Ladysmith via Pretoria* (London, 1900), opened to show a sketch of the prison in which he was held in Pretoria.
Rhodes House Library: 610.16 r.24

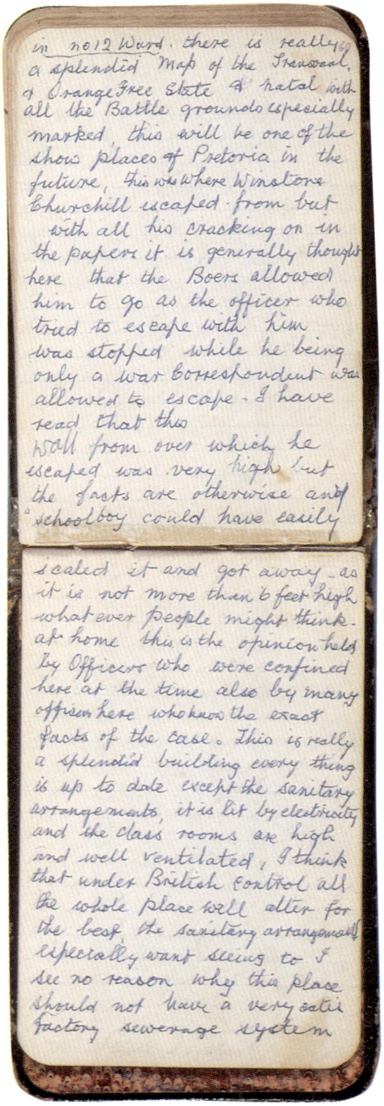

55 Diary of James Lowe, a baker with the British army in the Transvaal, opened to show his less heroic account of Churchill's escape.
Rhodes House Library: Mss. Afr. r.223

56 Photograph of James Lowe, *ca. 1900.*
Rhodes House Library: Mss. Afr. r.223

Africans and the Anglo-Boer War

Africans were intimately involved in all aspects of the conflict. Both sides used them as servants and drivers, as scouts and blockade runners, and in labour gangs to repair war damage. The British also armed some African tribes, especially in the north-west. During the war Africans reasserted control over land and livestock previously taken by the Boers, and on occasion attacked Boer commandos and settlements. In retaliation the Boers razed entire settlements to the ground and meted out severe punishments to any Africans found working for the British. In response, some British liberals and missionaries began to call for the Africans to be granted greater political rights after the end of the war.

57 Photograph of armed African auxiliaries, *ca. 1900.*
Rhodes House Library: Lee papers

55

58 Letter from Edward Garraway, a surgeon on military duties, to the Commanding Officer of the British South Africa Police, dated 10 May 1900, describing a raid by the Bakatla and their treatment of captured Boer civilians. Garraway's letter stresses that, contrary to the myth later propagated by the Afrikaners, the Bakatla treated their prisoners well, none of whom complained of the treatment they had received.
Rhodes House Library: Mss. Afr. s.1610/10 ff.1-2

59 Letter from Canon Farmer, Anglican missionary in Krugersdorp, Transvaal, dated 29 March 1900, in which he describes a raid by a Boer commando, led by Jan Smuts, on the village of Modderfontein during which all the Africans there were murdered and their bodies left unburied. According to Farmer, the Boers 'look upon the Kaffirs as dogs and the killing of them as hardly a crime'.
Rhodes House Library: U.S.P.G. papers E56a ff.319-323

60 Photograph of General Smuts during the Anglo-Boer war.
Rhodes House Library: Lee papers

61 Natives 'Flogging' Book, dated November 1901 to June 1902. Each entry gives the name of the culprit, his offence, the witnesses, the number of lashes awarded and by whom. The offences include breaking the curfew, refusing to obey orders, striking superior officers, escape from custody, drunkenness, cruelty to animals, spying, gambling, theft and insubordination.
Rhodes House Library: Mss. Afr. s.2323

62 South African Vigilance Committee. *The Black man and the war* (Cape Town, 1900).
Rhodes House Library: 610.16 r.160

Prisoners of War

The British sent many of the Boer prisoners of war to camps on St Helena or Ceylon.

63 Two photographs from the studio of A.L. Innes, Jamestown, of Boer prisoners of war on St Helena, 1902.
Rhodes House Library: Mss. Atlan. s.16

64 E.L. Jackson. *St. Helena: the historic island* (London, 1903), opened to show photographs of an escape attempt by a Boer prisoner of war.
Rhodes House Library: 940 r.8

65 J.N. Brink. *Recollections of a Boer prisoner-of-war at Ceylon* (Amsterdam, 1904).
Rhodes House Library: C99 R1030

66 Wooden letter opener made at Ragama camp, Ceylon, by a Boer prisoner of war, 1902.
Private collection

67 Medallion depicting the arms of the Transvaal made by J.E. O'Neill, when prisoner of war in Ceylon, dated 22 October 1901.
Private collection

Concentration camps

In order to deprive Boer commandos of supply the British evicted many Boer women and children from their farms and villages and sent them to concentration camps, where many died from malnutrition and disease. Many Black farm workers and ex-miners were also sent to 'refugee' camps, where they suffered even worse privations than the Boers. Following Emily Hobhouse's fact-finding mission and the subsequent investigation by Millicent Fawcett's Ladies' Commission, the scandal of the camps was exposed in Britain, leading the leader of the opposition Liberal Party, Campbell-Bannerman, to condemn the policy in his famous 'methods of barbarism' speech.

68 Photograph of a concentration camp, *ca.* 1901.
Rhodes House Library: Lee papers

69 Emily Hobhouse. *Report to the Committee of the Distress Fund for South African Women and Children* (London, 1901), opened to show some of the personal testimonies of camp inmates collected by Emily Hobhouse.
Rhodes House Library: 610.1 r.143 (22-23)

70 Emily Hobhouse. *The brunt of the war and where it fell* (London, 1902), opened to show a photograph of a child in the concentration camps.
Rhodes House Library: 610.16 r.28

Death of Cecil Rhodes

Cecil Rhodes died on 2 March 1902. Following a state funeral in Cape Town, his body was taken by train to Bulawayo, from where it was carried up into the Matopos Hills to be buried at the 'World's View', where it still remains.

71 Death mask of Cecil Rhodes. The original mould was made on the night Rhodes died and subsequently destroyed. It is thought that a total of eight copies were made, although the present location of all of them is not known.
Lent by the Rhodes Trust

72 Commemorative medal issued to those taking part in Rhodes' funeral, 1902.
Lent by the Rhodes Trust

73 Two photographs, showing Rhodes' body lying in state in Cape Town and the funeral train about to depart.
Rhodes House Library: Mss. Afr. t.45

74 Autograph copy of Rudyard Kipling's poem *C.J.R.*, which was read at Rhodes' graveside by the author, 10 April 1902.
Rhodes House Library: Mss. Afr. s.1772

The End of the Anglo-Boer War

The Boers reluctantly accepted peace terms from the British in May 1902 in the Treaty of Vereeniging. However, having lost the war, the Boers won the peace. Pressure from the British pro-Boers meant that the terms were generous, and, crucially, the question of the native franchise was deferred until after the grant of self-government. This effectively excluded the Africans from political power until almost the end of the century. They were also forced to return much of the land taken from the Boers during the war.

75 Cocoa cup and saucer commemorating end of the war, 1902.
Private collection

76 *United under the one flag*, handkerchief commemorating the end of the war and the incorporation of the Boer republics into a united South Africa under British rule, *ca.* 1902.
Private collection

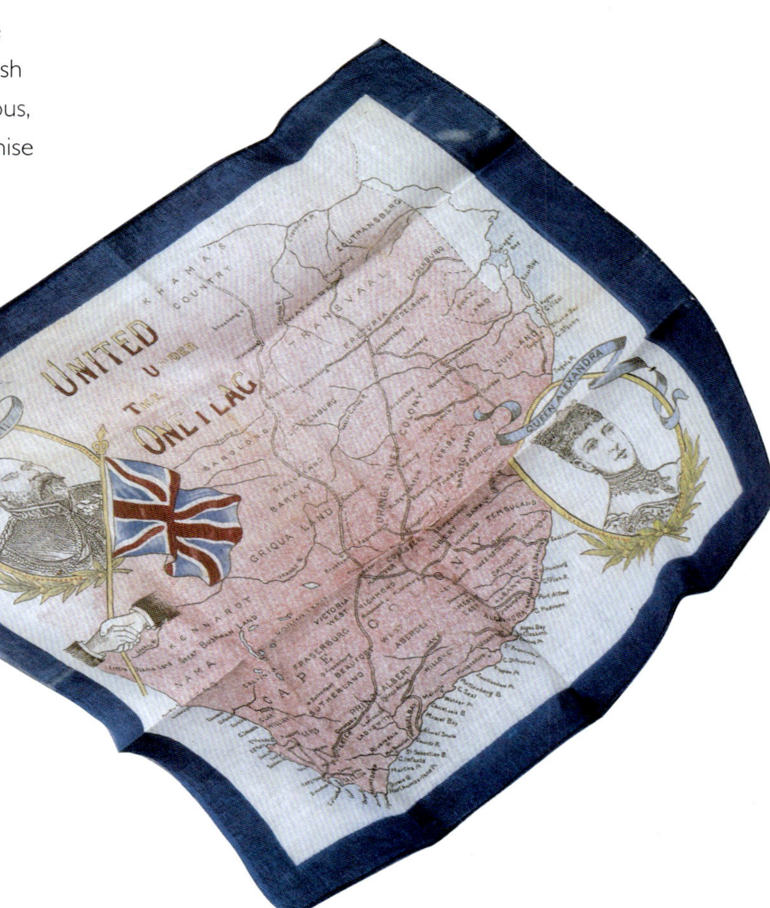

76

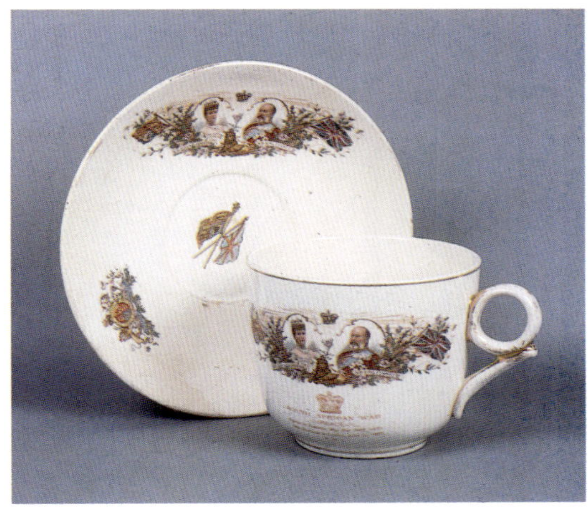

75

'Chinese Slavery'

Following the end of the Anglo-Boer War the mine-owners found there was a severe shortage of labour for the mines. They asked Milner to obtain labour for them from China and the first 10,000 workers arrived in South Africa in May 1904. Over a four-year period more than 63,000 Chinese were recruited and sent to the Rand, but their presence was bitterly resented by white workers. The Chinese were housed in compounds and the question of 'Chinese slavery' became a major issue in the British general election of 1906. The newly-elected Liberal government insisted on an end to the scheme and most of the workers were repatriated. Their presence, however, had the long-term effects of reducing wages for African workers and of their being housed in compounds too.

77 Three prints, taken from contemporary glass lantern slides, depicting Chinese labourers in the mine compounds, *ca.* 1906.
Rhodes House Library: U.S.P.G. lantern slides, box 6, nos. 21-23

78 *A Celestial vision*: cartoon in the Johannesburg *Sunday Times*, 24 June 1906, showing many of the leading personalities in South African society as Chinese figures. The mock Chinese names next to each figure can be linked to a well-known individual; thus Hi Kom is the High Commissioner, Lord Selborne, Ah Boo is Abe Bailey, Sol Jo is Solly Joel and so on.
Rhodes House Library: Mss. Afr. s.2175/8

79 Cartoon from *The Transvaal Critic*, 11 May 1906, expressing the mine-owners' concern at the ending of Chinese labour on the Rand.
Rhodes House Library: Mss. Afr. s.2175/8

80 Melanie Yap and Dianne Leong Man. *Colour, confusion and concessions: the history of the Chinese in South Africa* (Hong Kong, 1996), opened to show bunk room remains from the era of Chinese labour on the Rand.
Rhodes House Library: C96.S00349

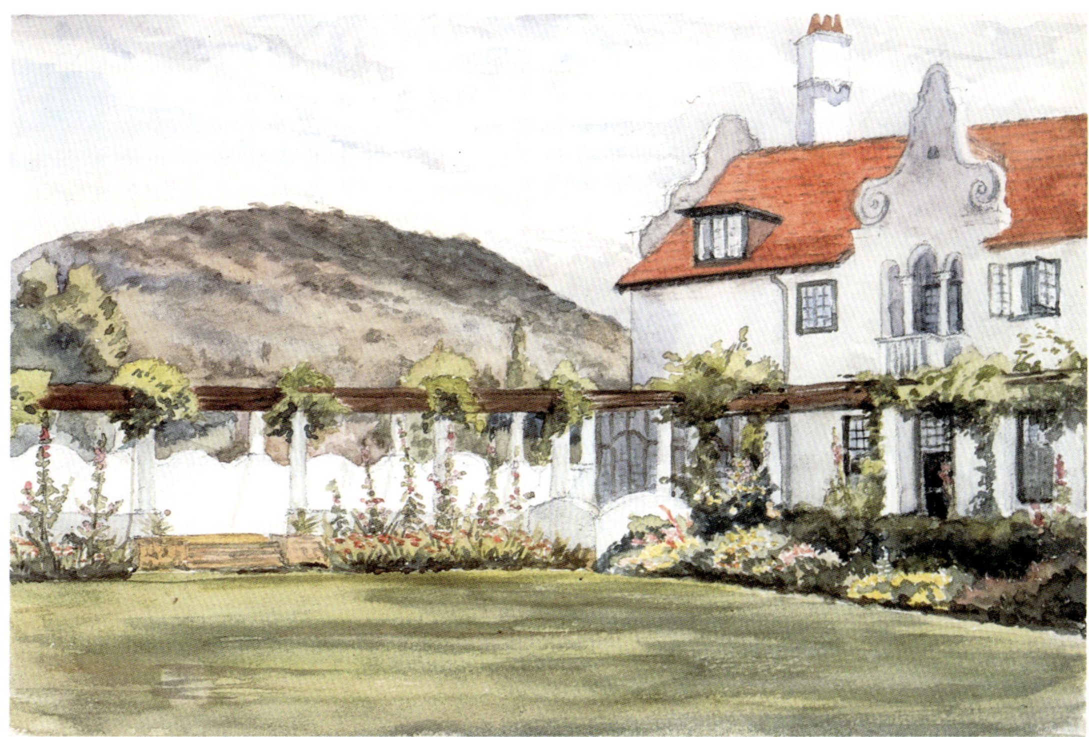

81

A Randlord's House

One of the mine-owners most keen to employ Chinese labour was Sir George Farrar. His house, Bedford Park, was designed by Sir Herbert Baker, and was typical of the houses the Randlords had built for themselves. Bedford Park still exists, but is now used to house a school.

81 Three watercolours of Bedford Park, *ca.*1905. *Rhodes House Library: Mss. Afr. s.2175/20/1*

The First World War

Many Afrikaners opposed South African participation on the side of the Allies in the First World War, and the government under General Botha had to suppress an armed Afrikaner Rebellion. South African troops were used to seize German South West Africa (Namibia), and over 20,000 South Africans served under Smuts in German East Africa (Tanzania). South Africa hoped to incorporate both these territories into the Union after the war, but although South West Africa was made a South African mandate under the League of Nations, German East Africa was administered by Britain after the war until independence.

82 Letter from Sir George Farrar to his wife, dated 20 September 1914, describing the difficult situation the South African government faced at the outbreak of war and how Botha dealt with it. Farrar later served as Quartermaster-General in South West Africa, and was killed in a railway accident there in 1915.
Rhodes House Library: Mss. Afr. s.2175/12/1

83 Three photographs of South African forces in German South West Africa, working to extend the railway and sinking new wells to supply the advancing troops with water. General Botha's visit to the railhead is also depicted. 1915.
Rhodes House Library: Mss. Afr. s.2175/12/2

84 Two volumes of diaries of Colonel Richard Meinertzhagen, who served as intelligence officer with the South African and British forces in East Africa. They record his opinion of Smuts as commander, of the South Africans in general and of their war aims.
Rhodes House Library: Meinertzhagen diaries, vols. 17 and 18

Red Revolt on the Rand, 1922

Economic depression in the mining industry in 1921 led many of the mining companies to propose cutting white workers' pay and recruiting Africans to do many jobs previously reserved for whites. The mine unions struck in protest in early 1922, and Afrikaner mineworkers organised themselves into commandos to enforce the strike. In response Smuts, as Prime Minister, declared martial law and sent in troops to crush the strike. After four days' fighting, in which over 150 people died, the strikers were defeated, and four of their leaders were subsequently executed. However, Smuts' brutal suppression of the strike was a contributory factor to his defeat in the 1924 election, and the new government took steps to restrict Africans to unskilled jobs.

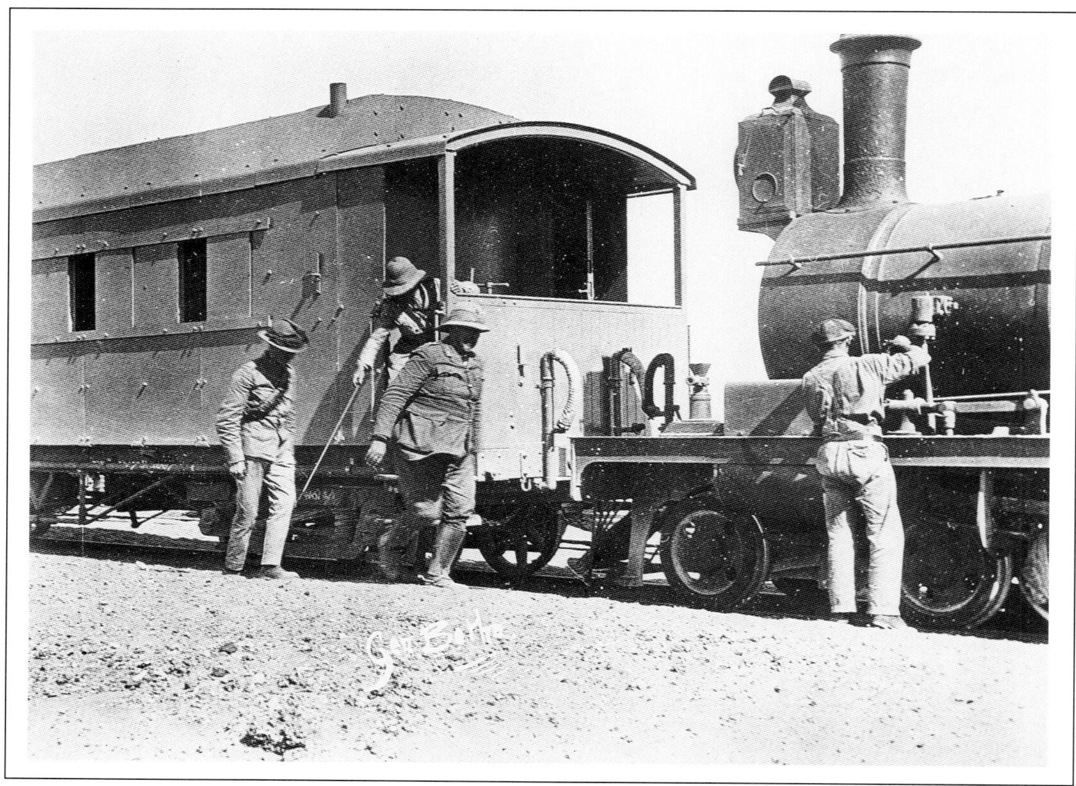

83

85 *Through the red revolt on the Rand: a pictorial review of events, January, February, March, 1922* (Johannesburg, 1922).
Rhodes House Library: 623.13 r.1(13)

86 Two letters from Jan Smuts to the Gillett family of Oxford, dated 23 February and 24 March 1922, giving Smuts' views on the strike and the measures he took to suppress it. The Gilletts were long-standing friends of Smuts and he wrote to them regularly from 1905 until just before his death.
Rhodes House Library: Mss. Afr. s.1414

Jan Christiaan Smuts

87 Soldier, naturalist, philosopher and international statesman, Smuts was the leading political figure of his generation in South Africa. Prime Minister from 1920 to 1924 and again from 1939 to 1948, he was also active on a wider political stage, serving in the Imperial War Cabinet during the First World War and playing a leading role in setting up the United Nations after the Second World War. Regarded as a liberal abroad (he counted Gandhi amongst his friends), at home he supported many measures which helped entrench racial segregation in South African society.

Portrait by J. Bodley.

Lent by the Rhodes Trust

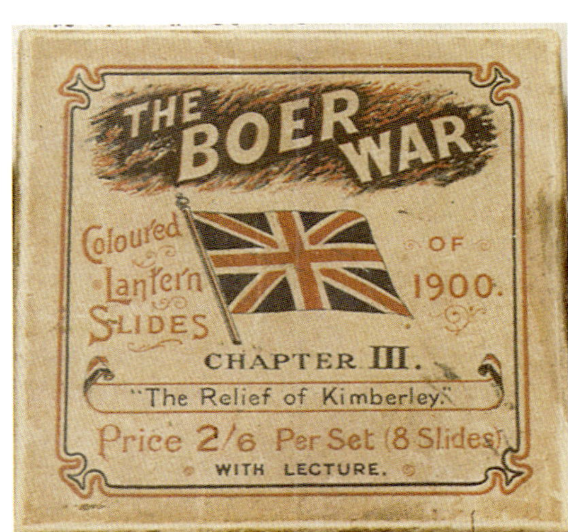

THE FREEDOM CHARTER

We the People of South Africa, declare for all our country and the world to know:- that South Africa belongs to all who live in it, black and white, and that no government can justly claim authority unless it is based on the will of the people; that our people have been robbed of their birthright to land, liberty and peace by a form of government founded on injustice and inequality; that our country will never be prosperous or free until all our people live in brotherhood, enjoying equal rights and opportunities; that only a democratic state, based on the will of all the people can secure to all their birthright without distinction of colour race sex or belief.

And therefore we, the People of South Africa, black and white together — equals countrymen and brothers — adopt this Freedom Charter. — And we pledge ourselves to strive together, sparing neither strength nor courage, until the democratic changes here set out have been won.

THE PEOPLE SHALL GOVERN!

Every man and woman shall have the right to vote for and to stand as a candidate for all bodies which make laws;

All people shall be entitled to take part in the administration of the country;

The rights of the people shall be the same, regardless of race colour or sex;

All bodies of a minority rule, advisory boards councils and authorities shall be replaced by democratic organs of self government.

ALL NATIONAL GROUPS SHALL HAVE EQUAL RIGHTS!

There shall be equal status in the bodies of the state, in the courts and in the schools for all national groups and races.

All people shall have equal right to use their own languages and to develop their own folk culture and customs.

All national groups shall be protected by law against insults to their race and national pride;

The preaching and practise of national, race or colour discrimination and contempt shall be a punishable crime.

All apartheid laws and practices shall be set aside.

THE PEOPLE SHALL SHARE IN THE COUNTRY'S WEALTH!

The national wealth of our country, the heritage of all South Africans, shall be restored to the people;

The mineral wealth beneath the soil, the banks and monopoly industry shall be transferred to the ownership of the people as a whole;

All other industry and trade shall be controlled to assist the wellbeing of the people;

All the people shall have equal rights to trade where they choose, to manufacture goods, and to enter all trades crafts and professions.

THE LAND SHALL BE SHARED AMONG THOSE WHO WORK IT!

Restriction of land ownership on a racial basis shall be ended, and all the land redivided among those who work it, to banish famine and land hunger;

The state shall help the peasants with implements, seed, tractors and dams to save the soil and assist the tillers.

Freedom of movement shall be guaranteed to all who work on the land;

All shall have the right to occupy land wherever they choose,

People shall not be robbed of their cattle, and forced labour and farm prisons shall be abolished.

ALL SHALL BE EQUAL BEFORE THE LAW!

No one shall be imprisoned deported or restricted without a fair trial;

No one shall be condemned by the order of any government official:—

The courts shall be representative of all the people;

Imprisonment shall be for serious crimes only committed against the people and shall aim at re-education not vengeance;

The police force and army shall be open to all on an equal basis and shall be the helpers and protectors of the people;

All laws which discriminate on grounds of race, colour or belief shall be repealed.

ALL SHALL ENJOY EQUAL HUMAN RIGHTS

The law shall guarantee to all their right to speak, to organise, to meet together, to publish, to preach, to worship and to educate their children;

The privacy of the house from police raids shall be protected by law:—

All shall be free to travel without restriction from countryside to town from province to province, and from South Africa abroad;

Pass laws, permits and all other laws restricting these freedoms shall be abolished.

THERE SHALL BE WORK AND SECURITY

All who work shall be free to form trade unions to elect their officers and to make wage agreements with their employers;

The state shall recognise the right and duty of all to work and to draw full unemployment benefits;

Men and women of all races shall receive equal pay for equal work;

There shall be a forty hour working week, a national minimum wage, paid annual leave and sick leave for all workers, and maternity leave on full pay for all working mothers;

Miners, domestic workers, farm workers and civil servants shall have the same rights as all others to work.

Child labour, compound labour the tot system and contract labour shall be abolished.

THE DOORS OF LEARNING AND CULTURE SHALL BE OPENED

The government shall discover, develop and encourage national talent for the enhancement of our cultural life.

All cultural treasures of mankind shall be open to all, by free exchange of books, ideas and contact with other lands;

The aim of education shall be to teach the youth to love their people and their culture, to honour human brotherhood, liberty and peace;

Education shall be free, compulsory, universal and equal for all children.

Higher education and technical training shall be opened to all by means of state allowances and scholarships awarded on the basis of merit.

Adult illiteracy shall be ended by a mass state education plan;

Teachers shall have the rights of other citizens.

The colour bar in cultural life, in sport and in education shall be abolished.

THERE SHALL BE HOUSES SECURITY AND COMFORT

All people shall have the right to live where they choose, to be decently housed, and to bring up their families in comfort and security.

Unused housing space to be made available to the people;

Rent and prices shall be lowered food plentiful and no one shall go hungry;

A preventive health scheme shall be run by the state;

Free medical care and hospitalization shall be provided for all, with special care for mothers and young children.

Slums shall be demolished, and new suburbs built where all have transport, roads, lighting, playing fields, crèches and social centres.

The aged, the orphans, the disabled and the sick shall be cared for by the state;

Rest leisure and recreation shall be the right of all.

Fenced locations and ghettoes shall be abolished and laws which break up families shall be repealed.

THERE SHALL BE PEACE AND FRIENDSHIP

South Africa shall be a fully independent state which respects the rights and sovereignty of all nations.

South Africa shall strive to maintain world peace and the settlement of all international disputes by negotiation not war.

Peace and friendship amongst all our people shall be secured by upholding the equal rights, opportunities and status of all,

The people of the protectorates:-

—Basutoland, Bechuanaland and Swaziland—

shall be free to decide for themselves their own future;

The right of the peoples of Africa to Independence and self government shall be recognised and shall be the basis of close co-operation.

Adopted at the Congress of The People at Kliptown Johannesburg on June 25 and 26, 1955.

LET ALL WHO LOVE THEIR PEOPLE AND THEIR COUNTRY NOW SAY AS WE SAY HERE — "THESE FREEDOMS WE WILL FIGHT FOR SIDE BY SIDE, THROUGHOUT OUR LIVES UNTIL WON OUR — LIBERTY!"

Presented to Tsitwalandwe Huddleston by the A.N.C.Y.L., C.O.D.Y., T.I.Y.C., SACPO.Y.

by Marion Frenry

THE RISE AND FALL OF APARTHEID

White supremacy of one kind or another had been present in South Africa since it was first settled by the Dutch, but 'segregation' in its recognizably 'modern' form only emerged during and after Milner's postwar 'reconstruction' of the Transvaal. Segregation's essence was the mobilization and control of cheap African labour. Following recommendations by the South African Native Affairs Commission of 1903-05, laws were passed which over the course of several decades imposed a colour bar, segregated land ownership and established separate African townships. In the 1940s, however, segregation began to break down under the pressure of large-scale African urbanization. For many Afrikaners, especially workers threatened by black competition for jobs and farmers anxious to secure continued supplies of rightless African labourers, it seemed that their interests could only be safeguarded by the National Party's promise of Apartheid.

Yet in 1948 when the National Party came to power, Apartheid was far from being a coherent ideology. Beyond keeping power in white hands and a general desire to separate the 'races', there was little agreement among its supporters.

But as policy evolved during the 1950s and 1960s, so successive acts tightened the whites' grip on the state, all the time enforcing the classification of the country's population into four 'racial' categories: Black, Coloured, Indian and White. Measures such as the Group Areas Act of 1950 were extended to apply segregation to every aspect of social life, including the entrances of public buildings, beaches, lifts, restaurants and even libraries, where blacks and whites had to read books at separate tables. Coloureds and Indians also suffered under this legislation.

The implementation of Apartheid was resisted whenever possible. The 1950s not only witnessed rural protest and the African National Congress' Defiance Campaign, but also the Freedom Charter adopted at Kliptown in June 1955. While its commitment to redivide the land 'amongst those who work it' and to 'public ownership of mines and banks' was too much for the Liberal Party to swallow, it was not sufficiently Africanist for those militants who in 1959 broke away to form the Pan-Africanist Congress. It was the refusal of PAC members to carry passes which precipitated the Sharpeville Massacre of March 1960, in which 69 people were shot dead by the police. Probably more than any other single act, this state-sanctioned murder aroused international condemnation of Apartheid.

But with most Western countries still reluctant to impose sanctions, South Africa enjoyed high rates of economic growth for much of the 1960s. Ignoring the 'winds of change' sweeping through the rest of the continent, South Africa's rulers dealt ruthlessly with their opponents. The same decade also saw the strict enforcement of influx control measures as the Bantustan strategy of establishing so-called 'ethnic homelands' for Africans was implemented. Between *ca.* 1960 and the mid-1980s some 3.7 million people were forcibly removed in order to give effect to Group Areas and Separate Development legislation.

Confident in its ability to have its own way, the Apartheid state brushed aside warnings that the planned teaching in Afrikaans of half the curriculum in African schools would ignite unrest. The resulting explosion was the Soweto rising of 1976, in which protesting school pupils were joined by embittered youth rendered unemployable by lack of training and a severe downturn in the economy. Although the unrest

was brutally suppressed, it marked the beginning of a new era of mass resistance. In August 1983 the United Democratic Front, an umbrella body sympathetic to the ANC, was formed. Even so, popular feelings frequently outpaced political organizations. What began as a rent boycott in industrial townships south of Johannesburg in September 1984 soon engulfed other urban areas. Violent protest was fuelled by the ruthlessness with which the state responded.

Eventually thousands of people were killed. By the end of the decade the Apartheid authorities had succeeded in clamping a lid on mass struggle. While they could not end it they could contain it.

But the South African government had been far less successful in arresting the country's precipitous economic decline. South Africa's gross domestic product had not only stopped growing, it was actually shrinking. This economic crisis greatly undermined the regime's capacity to withstand external pressure, not least in 1987 when the United States and the then Soviet Union brokered a peace settlement in Angola and Namibia. Yet this was also far from being unequivocally in the interests of the ANC. As part of the deal, it had to vacate its Angolan bases. Both sides, then, were ready to negotiate as the 1980s drew to a close. In February 1990 the ANC and the South African Communist Party were 'unbanned' by the South African government, and Nelson Mandela released from twenty-seven years' imprisonment. Following protracted negotiations, the country's first democratic elections were held in April 1994.

The Freedom Charter

The Freedom Charter was adopted by a meeting of the Congress of the People at Kliptown in June 1955. It demanded a non-racial democratic government, and as such became a rallying point, not just for the African National Congress, which adopted it as a statement of principles in 1956, but of the majority of black South Africans.

88 Facsimile of an illuminated copy of the Freedom Charter, presented to Trevor Huddleston when he left South Africa, 1956.
Rhodes House Library: Anti-Apartheid Movement papers

The Introduction of Apartheid

Racial segregation had been present in South Africa since it was first settled by the Dutch, but Apartheid was only introduced piecemeal following the National Party's victory in the general election of 1948 and especially after Dr. Verword became Prime Minister. Among early attempts to resist Apartheid was a campaign of passive resistance by the Indian community in Natal, which was inspired by the similar campaigns waged by Gandhi in India.

89 Johannesburg District Committee of the Communist Party. *Malanazi menace* (Johannesburg, 1948).
Rhodes House Library: Pam 613 r. COM

90 *Passive resister*, the newspaper of the Natal Indian Congress, opened to show an address by the Rev. Michael Scott.
Rhodes House Library: C93. T15/16

91 Mohan Kumaramangalam. *Indians fight for equality in South Africa* (Bombay, 1946).
Rhodes House Library: Pam 613 r.KUM

Two pamphlets by Dr. Verwoerd, Prime Minister of South Africa, 1958-1966, and chief architect of Apartheid:

92 *Separate development: the positive side*
(Pretoria, 1958).
Rhodes House Library: 610.43 r.73(2)

93 *Last steps to the Republic of South Africa*
(Bloemfontein, 1960).
Rhodes House Library: 610.43 r.73(1)

94 Letter from Dr. Verwoerd to A.J. Culwick, a
British settler in Kenya, dated 13 August 1960,
outlining his policies.
Rhodes House Library: Culwick papers

95 Ambrose Reeves. *Shooting at Sharpeville: the
agony of South Africa* (London, 1960), opened to
show two photographs of victims of the
massacre.
Rhodes House Library: 623.12 r.40

Trevor Huddleston and South Africa

Trevor Huddleston, a member of the Community
of the Resurrection, ministered to people of the
black townships of the Rand between 1943 and
1956. An outspoken opponent of Apartheid,
he witnessed and tried to prevent the forced
removals from Sophiatown, Johannesburg. His
book *Naught for your comfort* was instrumental
in raising awareness of the evils of Apartheid to
a whole generation in Europe and North
America, and in later years he served as an
inspirational chairman of the Anti-Apartheid
Movement in Britain.

Following the publication of *Naught for your
comfort*, Alexander Steward was commissioned
to write a rather half-hearted riposte, entitled
You are wrong Father Huddleston.

96 Photograph of Trevor Huddleston in
Sophiatown, 1950s.
Rhodes House Library: Huddleston papers

97 Trevor Huddleston. *Naught for your comfort*
(London, 1956).
Rhodes House Library: 610.422 r.13

98 Alexander Steward. *You are wrong Father
Huddleston* (London, 1956).
Rhodes House Library: 610.422 r.14

Harold Macmillan and 'The wind of change'

In January-February 1960 the British Prime
Minister, Harold Macmillan, made a tour of Africa,
which culminated in his speech to the South
African Parliament on 3 February. It was a speech
into which a great deal of thought, by numerous
people, had been put over the previous two or

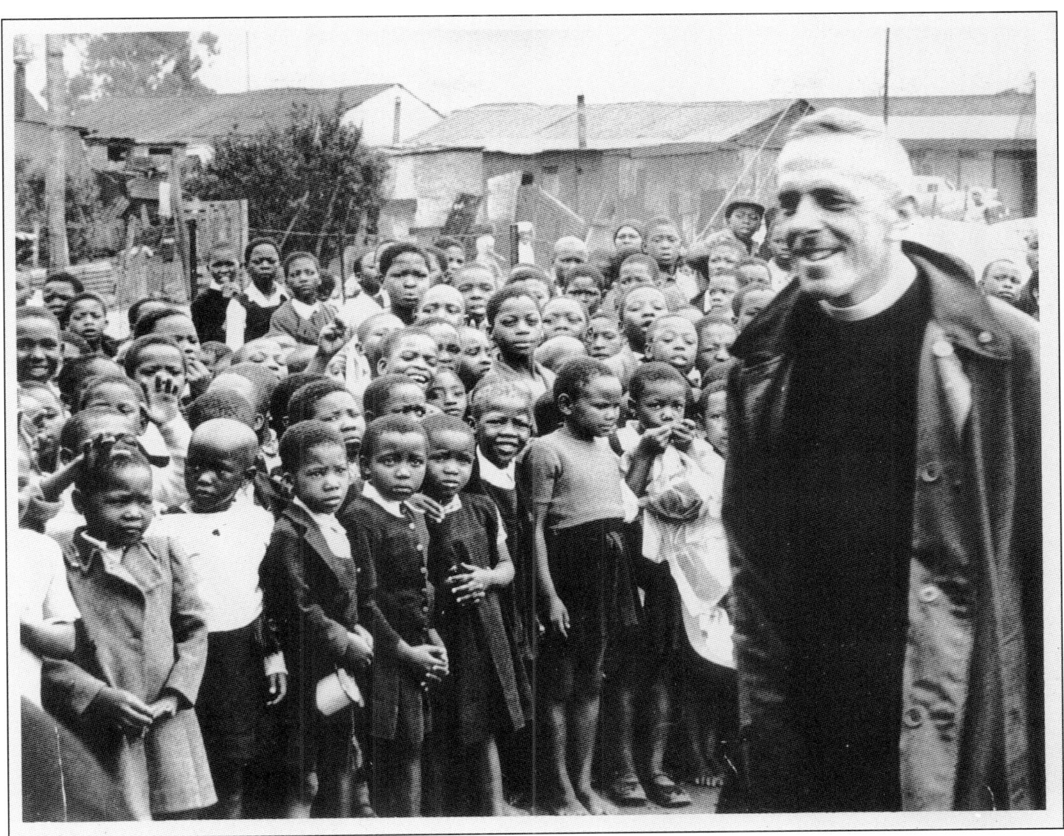

96

three months and it was being worked on and amended right up until the night before it was delivered. Known from that day as the 'Wind of change' speech, it was a major recognition of the forces of African nationalism and a trenchant, although subtle, attack on the policy of Apartheid.

99 Draft copy of the speech, showing the addition of the phrase 'wind of change' in Macmillan's hand, and his speaking copy of the final text 'not quite as delivered', 1960.
Bodleian Library: MS. Macmillan dep. C788

Nelson Mandela and the Treason Trials

Nelson Mandela was one of the defendants in the long-running treason trials, which lasted from 1957 to 1961. Acquitted, he was then instrumental in founding the new military wing of the African National Congress, known as Umkhonto we Sizwe. Following the arrest of a group of Umkhonto we Sizwe leaders at Rivonia, near Johannesburg, in 1962, he was charged with sabotage and planning guerrilla warfare and armed invasion of South Africa and was sentenced to life imprisonment. In prison on the notorious Robben Island, he became an icon for the resistance movement in South Africa and the anti-Apartheid movement worldwide.

100 Nelson Mandela. *I accuse: speeches to court.* (n.p., 1962). This copy was printed clandestinely in South Africa and was intended to be circulated in order to publicise Mandela's speeches in court, which were not reported by most South African newspapers.
Rhodes House Library: 610.5 r.48(16)

The Apartheid Era

The implementation of the Group Areas Act led to mass forced removals of people from their homes, and the razing to the ground of entire areas of housing. The results can clearly be seen in these 'before and after' photographs of District Six, Cape Town.

101 Cloete Breytenbach and Brian Barrow. *The spirit of District Six* (Cape Town, 1997).
Rhodes House Library: C99.S00152

102 Watercolour sketches of South African scenes by Phoebe Somers, 1962.
Rhodes House Library: Mss Afr. s.2162 (1/7) and (1/8)

103 During Apartheid all blacks had to carry a pass book, such as this one, which belonged to Samson Chauke, a member of staff of the Brenthurst Library, Johannesburg.
Rhodes House Library: Mss. Afr. s.2291

Many whites continued to support the policy of Apartheid, partly because they accepted National Party propaganda which equated African nationalism with Communism. As the National Party leadership began to realise that Apartheid was both counter-productive and ultimately unsustainable, some right-wingers seceded from the N.P. to found the Konserwatiewe/ Conservative Party, which continued to campaign for full political separation between white and black states in South Africa.

104 Flyer advertising an anti-Communist rally in East London, 31 October 1975.
Rhodes House Library: Culwick papers

105 *Political partition – the peaceful alternative.* Pamphlet of the Konserwatiewe Party, *ca.*1985.
Rhodes House Library: Culwick papers

A selection of anti-government papers published both inside and outside South Africa during the 1970s and '80s.

106 *UDF news: national newsletter of the United Democratic Front.*
Rhodes House Library: DT 31

107 *Grassroots: the paper about you.*
Rhodes House Library: DT 30

108 *Sechaba: official organ of the African National Congress.*
Rhodes House Library: 610.43 s.31

109 *Resister: bulletin of the Committee on South African War Resistance.*
Rhodes House Library: Anti-Apartheid Movement papers

The Anti-Apartheid Movement in Britain

For almost four decades, the Anti-Apartheid Movement campaigned in Britain for the end of Apartheid in South Africa. It had its origins in the Boycott Movement formed in London in 1959, in response to calls from the African National Congress for an international boycott of South African goods. The Boycott Movement organised a Boycott Month in March 1960, beginning with a mass rally in Trafalgar Square. Following the Sharpeville massacre on 21 March, it resolved to continue campaigning and transformed itself into the Anti-Apartheid Movement.

The AAM called for sports, cultural and economic boycotts, continued the boycott of consumer goods, lobbied for international disinvestment from South Africa and campaigned against military and nuclear collaboration. It organised many campaigns on behalf of political prisoners, including Nelson Mandela. The Movement also promoted independence for Namibia and the Portuguese colonies of Angola and Mozambique and campaigned against the illegal Smith regime in Rhodesia.

The AAM operated through a network of local groups and established contacts with South Africans in exile and anti-Apartheid groups in other countries. It lobbied the British government, the Commonwealth and the United Nations.

The AAM dissolved itself in 1995, following South Africa's first democratic elections, and transferred its archives to Rhodes House Library.

110 The items on display are a selection of the campaign materials produced by the AAM, and include the first issue of its monthly newspaper *Anti-Apartheid News*, January 1965.
Rhodes House Library: Anti-Apartheid Movement papers

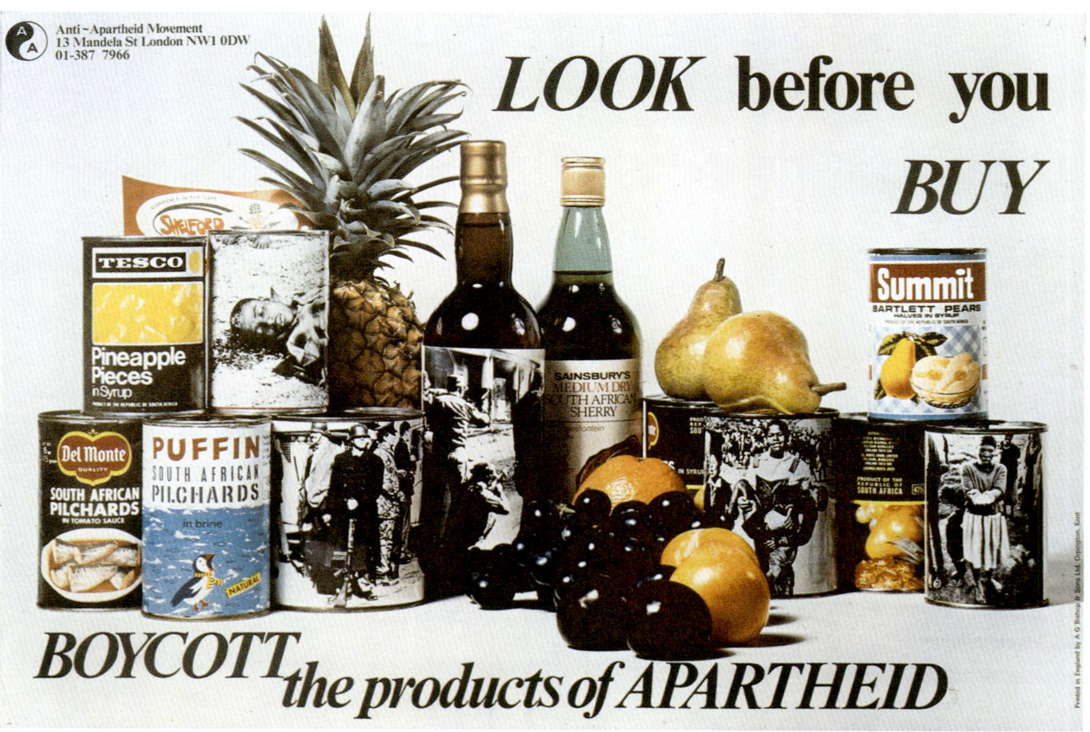

110

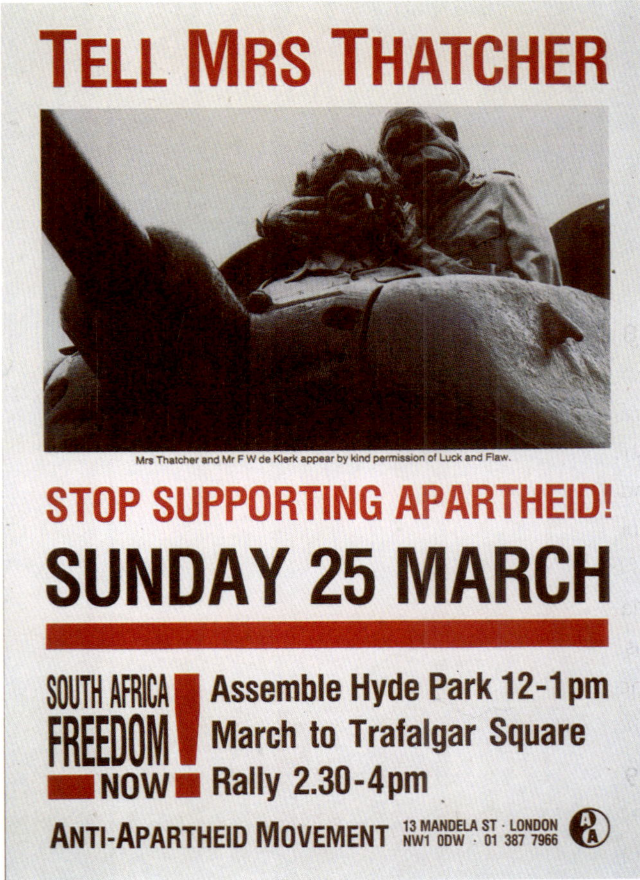

TELL MRS THATCHER
Mrs Thatcher and Mr F W de Klerk appear by kind permission of Luck and Flaw.
STOP SUPPORTING APARTHEID!
SUNDAY 25 MARCH
SOUTH AFRICA FREEDOM NOW!
Assemble Hyde Park 12-1pm
March to Trafalgar Square
Rally 2.30-4pm
ANTI-APARTHEID MOVEMENT
13 MANDELA ST · LONDON NW1 0DW · 01 387 7966

110

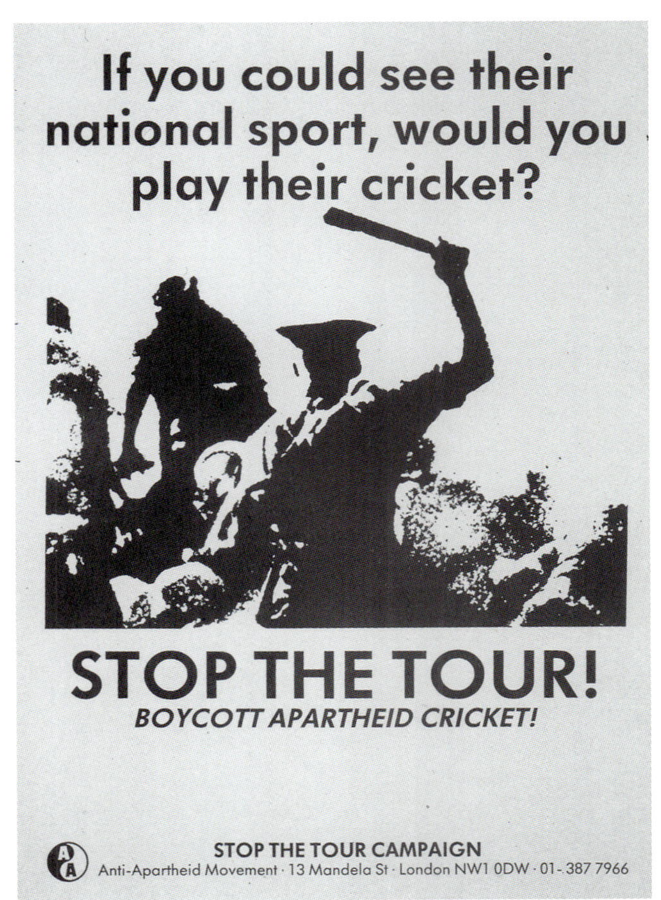

If you could see their national sport, would you play their cricket?
STOP THE TOUR!
BOYCOTT APARTHEID CRICKET!
STOP THE TOUR CAMPAIGN
Anti-Apartheid Movement · 13 Mandela St · London NW1 0DW · 01- 387 7966

110

Women Making Links Against Apartheid

111   Anti-Apartheid Movement banner, 1980s.

Rhodes House Library: Anti-Apartheid Movement papers

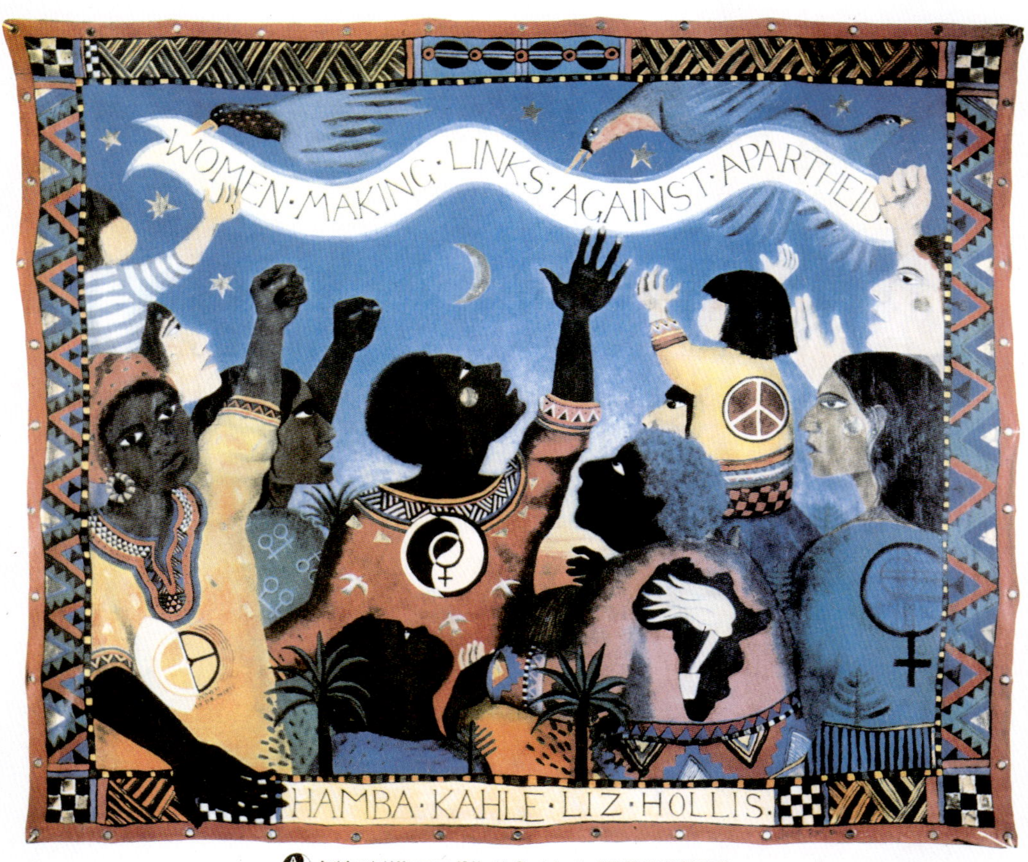

111

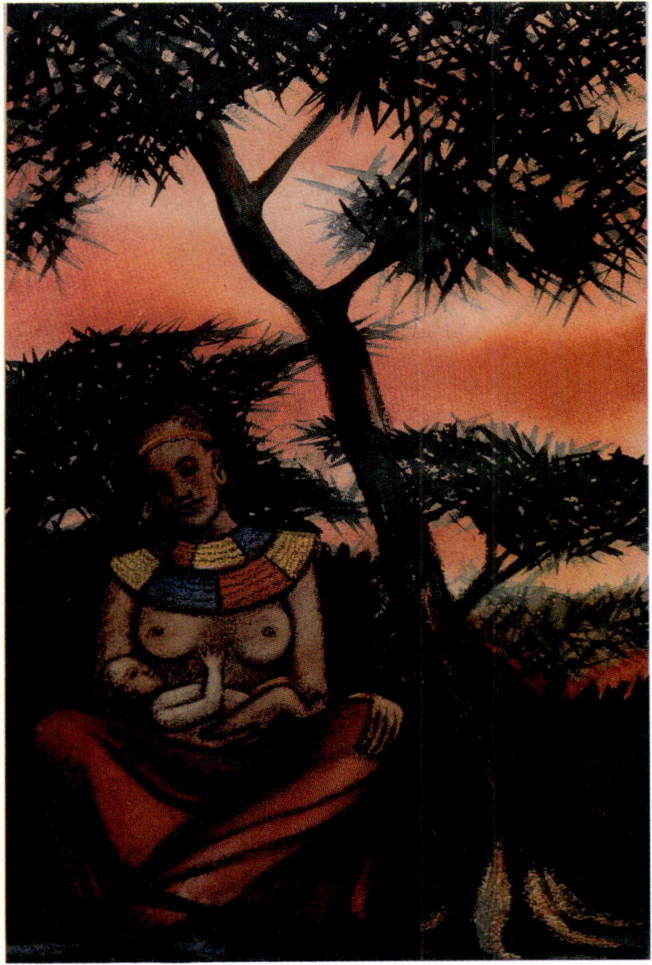

112

Annie Catford

112   Three pictures in pastel, charcoal and watercolour of imaginary South African scenes, 1988. They were designed to be used as cards to be sold in aid of the Anti-Apartheid Movement's campaign for the release of Nelson Mandela.
Rhodes House Library: Anti-Apartheid Movement papers

The End of Apartheid

As a result both of increasing internal resistance to Apartheid and of external economic pressures, especially after the United States Congress voted to impose sanctions against South Africa, the National Party government realised that the system could no longer be maintained. President De Klerk's speech of 27 February 1990 promised the unbanning of the liberation movements and the unconditional release of all political prisoners, including Nelson Mandela. This led to multiparty talks at the World Trade Centre, near Johannesburg, from 1991 to 1993, as a result of which a transitional constitution was agreed, and the way was paved for genuine democratic elections to take place in 1994.

113 Salt and pepper pots representing four of the key players in South African politics during the transitional periods: Archbishop Desmond Tutu, President F.W. De Klerk, Nelson Mandela and Eugene Terre'Blanche, founder of the right-wing Afrikaner Weerstandsbeweging, which campaigned for an independent Afrikaner homeland.
Private collection

114 *10 Commandments for Voters.* Poster produced by Project Vote for the 1994 elections.
Rhodes House Library: Mss. Afr, s.2176/22/13

115 African National Congress. *Let the people decide: negotiations and the struggle for a democratic South Africa* (Johannesburg, 1991).
Rhodes House Library: Pam 613 r.23

116 Flag of the new South Africa, 1994.
Rhodes House Library: Mss. Afr. s.2176/17/1

117 Copies of the *Sowetan* newspaper for 18 and 19 November 1993, recording the reaching of agreement on an interim constitution at the multiparty talks.
Rhodes House Library: DT 12

118 *Constitution of the Republic of South Africa Bill, 1996* (Pretoria, 1996). Copy signed by Nelson Mandela.
Rhodes House Library. Closed Bay (Mandela)

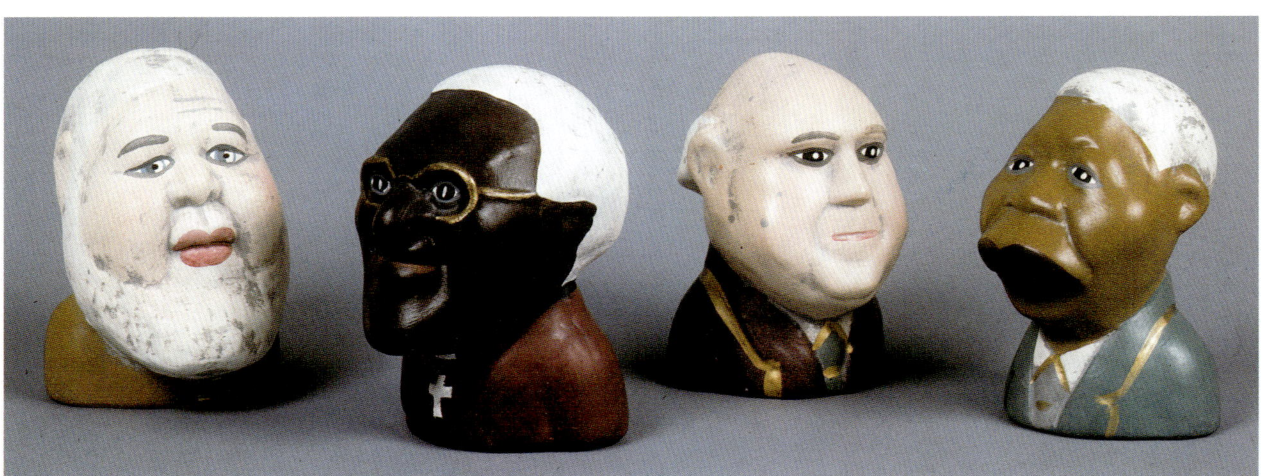

113

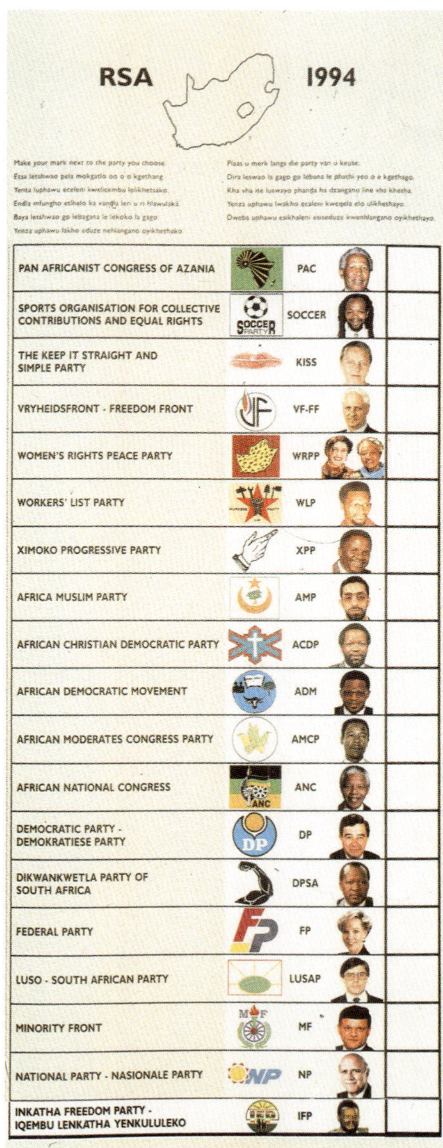

119

South African Elections, April 1994

In April 1994 the first multiracial and fully-democratic elections were held in South Africa, and a Government of National Unity, in which the African National Congress was the senior partner, was formed, with Nelson Mandela as State President.

119   The items on display are a representative sample of the wide-ranging and voluminous campaign materials produced by the nineteen parties who contested the elections, together with material produced by some of the bodies charged with voter education and with the conduct of the elections. Note that on the ballot paper the Inkatha Freedom Party has been added on a separate slip pasted in at the bottom of the list; this was because the IFP only decided to contest the election at a very late stage, when the ballot papers had already been printed. *Rhodes House Library: Mss. Afr. s.2176*

The photographs of the election are by Oxford resident Helen Kimble, who was an Election Monitor.

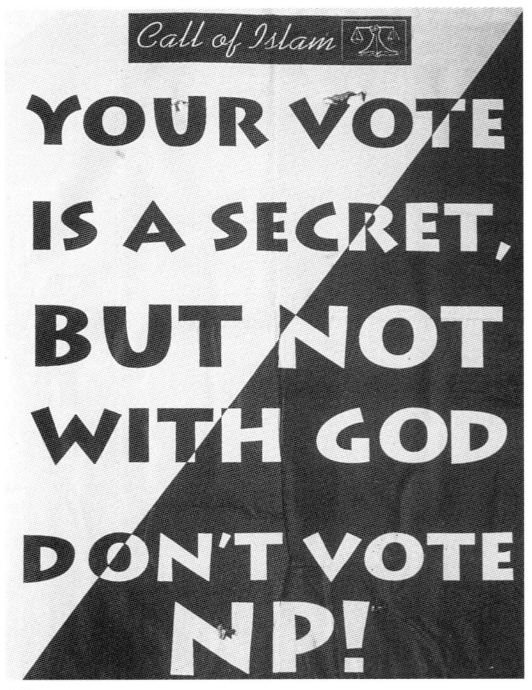

119

120   Independent Electoral Commission.
Banner from a polling station, 1994.
Rhodes House Library: Mss. Afr. s.2176

121   *Poll result today.* Argus poster, 1994.
Rhodes House Library: Mss. Afr. s.2176

Nelson Mandela

Following the 1994 elections Nelson Mandela
was sworn in as first President of a democratic
South Africa.

122   African National Congress poster from
the 1994 elections.
Rhodes House Library: Mss. Afr. s.2176/18

123   Bust of Nelson Mandela.
*Rhodes House Library: Anti-Apartheid
Movement papers*

In 1996 the University of Oxford conferred the
Degree of Civil Law by Diploma on President
Mandela. The following year he visited Oxford to
be received by the University and to deliver an
address entitled *Renewal and renaissance: towards
a new world order* under the auspices of the
Oxford Centre for Islamic Studies.

124   Text of the Diploma.
Rhodes House Library: Mss. Afr. t.54

125   Nelson Mandela. *Renewal and renaissance:
towards a new world order* (Oxford, 1997).
Signed copy.
Rhodes House Library: C97. R628
[unsigned copy]

Bibliography

Brian Barker. *A concise dictionary of the Boer War*
(Cape Town, 1999)

William Beinart. *Twentieth-century South Africa*
(Oxford, 1994)

T.R.H. Davenport. *The transfer of power in South Africa*
(Cape Town, 1998)

Christabel Gurney. *'A great cause': the origins of the
Anti-Apartheid Movement, June 1959-June 1960*
(London, 1998)

Trevor Huddleston. *Naught for your comfort*
(London, 1956)

Peter Joyce. *A concise dictionary of South African
biography*
(Cape Town, 1999)

Nelson Mandela. *Long walk to freedom*
(London, 1994)

Bill Nasson. *The South African War, 1899-1902*
(London, 1999)

Pieter Oosthuizen. *Boer War memorabilia*
(Edmonton, 1987)

Thomas Pakenham. *The Boer War*
(London, 1979)

John Pinfold. 'Archives in Oxford relating to the South
African War', *African research and documentation* 79
(1999)

Christopher Saunders. *Historical dictionary of South
Africa*
(Metuchen, N.J., 1983)

Iain Smith. *The origins of the South African War,
1899-1902*
(London, 1996)